A Park for E\

Contents

Everyone Loves a Park

Take a walk through this city park and you'll see how popular it is. There are children riding bicycles, parents pushing strollers, and young athletes playing soccer and baseball. There are also many people with dogs.

This is a park for everyone. But it hasn't always been this way.

The Problem with Dogs

Ten years ago, the park looked very different. There was graffiti everywhere, the grass was patchy, and only a few flowers grew. The park was run-down.

City dogs that live in apartments need space to play and exercise.

Not many people used the park besides people with dogs. These people came every day to exercise their dogs and themselves.

Over the next few years, the city began
fixing up the park. Also, park officials started
patrolling the grounds to make the park safer.
As a result, more people visited the park and
enjoyed their favorite activities.

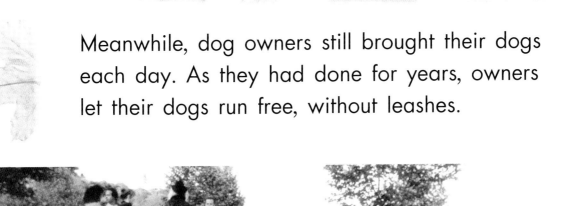

Meanwhile, dog owners still brought their dogs each day. As they had done for years, owners let their dogs run free, without leashes.

7

Some park visitors began to complain that dogs were becoming a problem.

"My child was knocked down by a dog running loose," complained one young mother.

"Dogs dig up the flowers and grass," said another park visitor.

"We can't go for a walk in peace," an elderly couple grumbled.

But dogs and dog owners also had needs.

Park Visitor Complaints

- Dogs are noisy and wild.

- Dogs dig up grass and gardens.

- Dogs make messes.

- Dogs scare away birds and wildlife.

Dog and Dog Owner Needs

- Dogs need exercise.

- Dogs need a place to play with other dogs.

- City dogs need space because they don't have backyards.

- Dogs need to use parks so they don't make messes on sidewalks.

9

Park officials began fining dog owners for not obeying the "leash law." This law says that dogs in the park must be on a leash at all times.

Park officials had rarely fined people before the park was fixed up. The city didn't think there was a problem then.

But off-leash dogs became a problem when many new visitors wanted to use the park.

Some park visitors were scared of dogs, especially dogs that were not leashed.

Leash Laws

Many cities and states have laws about where a dog needs to be on a leash. Different places have different rules, but some common ones are:

- Dogs in public areas, including parks, must be leashed at all times.

- A leash must be under a certain length (in many places, no longer than 6 feet).

- Dogs in their own yards must be held back by a fence, leash, or chain.

- Dogs must not be able to reach the public sidewalk if tied out in their yard.

- Dog owners who disobey the leash laws may be fined.

Dog Owners Form a Group

"Where can our dogs play and get exercise now?" dog owners wondered.

Many of them felt that something had to be done to help their dogs.

Dog owners talked with each other in the park day after day. Finally, they decided to form a group to deal with the problem.

Since so many people brought their dogs to the park every day, it was easy for them to form a group.

People in the group had different ideas about what they wanted for their dogs.

Some members of the group thought dogs should be allowed to play in the park's open meadows. But many open areas were being closed off to dogs because people wanted to use them.

Open areas were becoming playing fields, gardens, and picnic areas.

Other members thought an enclosed place just for dogs—a dog run—would be the best solution. After talking for a long time, the whole group agreed on this solution.

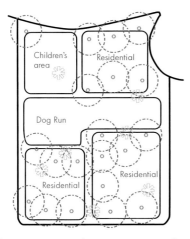

The group chose a good site for the dog run. Then they drew up a plan.

What Does a Good Dog Run Site Need?

- ☑ Source of drinking water
- ☑ Drainage
- ☑ Mix of shade and sun
- ☑ Place for small, shy dogs
- ☑ Parking (if most users drive to the dog run)

15

Solving the Problem Together

The dog owners showed their plan to city park officials and other community groups.

The dog owners explained how they had chosen their site and how they would maintain it.

Sports groups wanted space for fields.

As expected, other community groups had their own interests such as playing sports, bird-watching, and gardening.

"Why should dogs get that space when so many people want to use it in other ways?" asked the people from the other groups.

17

Everyone took time to discuss the problem and to listen to one another's ideas. In the end, they all agreed a dog run was a good solution.

There was give-and-take on everyone's part. The dog run would be built on the chosen site, which pleased the dog owners. But it would be smaller than first planned, which pleased the other community groups.

Local children helped to build the dog run.

18

Arguments for Dog Run	Arguments against Dog Run	Agreement
A dog run restricts off-leash dogs to one part of the park.	A dog run takes up space.	Space was allowed for the dog run, though not as much as dog owners asked for.
A dog run limits mess in other parts of the park.	A dog run is smelly and messy.	Dog owners group agreed to keep dog run clean and well drained.
A dog park limits crime in the area because people are around to keep watch.	A dog park is noisy and busy.	Dog owners agreed to control barking and noise.

After the dog run was built, the dog owners agreed to manage it themselves and to enforce certain park rules for the dog run. They

also added a few more rules of their own. These rules would help solve problems that might come up inside the dog run.

Common rules for a dog run:

1. Only those dogs that have licenses and have had all their shots may use the run.

2. Dogs must wear licenses and tags on their collars, which should be flat, not spiked.

3. Dog owners must always clean up after their dogs.

4. Dog owners must watch their dogs at all times and control them when needed.

RULES

- All dogs must be under voice restraint at all times.
- Dog owners are responsible for collecting and removing their dog's waste.
- Dog owners are responsible for their dog's behavior at all times.

21

Take a walk by the dog run today. It's a favorite place for dogs and dog owners. Because the dog run is well maintained, other park visitors have no complaints.